Poli-tics Spaceships 'n' Morphics

by

George Howard

Introduction

This is a compilation of short stories and poetry, specifically aimed at people coming into consciousness.

I have once again tried to keep a mix of humour and reality

People who are just coming to realise what's happening as well as people who are 'awake', will I hope enjoy this book.

David Icke is a hero of mine, and he is at last beginning to get the respect and recognition he deserves. He has been trying to wake people up for years.

More power to 'The People's Voice', and I hope you enjoy.

ISBN 978-1-291-47911-9

Spring Forth

The sun, once more awakening dawn choristers.
Songbirds, sweet music, to make the genius composer weep.
Strolling once more down lanes, sentries of Hawthorn and Privet.
Now in uniforms new, garbs in shades of emerald.
Lawns and pavements once more covered white,
Carpeted with petal confetti, leaving cherries blushing, naked, behind,
Blades of lush new green, pushing defiantly forth with jubilance,
To greet the newly awakening world, of birth and growth.
Humming workers, dressed in black and yellow sweaters,
Tireless and urgent, one track minded unselfish wonders.
Unwittingly, spreading procreation, and thus joy to all,
Blossoms of incalculable variations of hues, colouring hedgerows,
Fields and gardens, sweet scents, aromas fit for Gods.
Babbling brooks, tumbling into limpid pools, teeming with life renewed,
Gondolas of white lilies, hosting croaking Gondoliers.
Lambs pulled swiftly into a glittering world,
Milking stool gait, unsteady and unsure.
Startled woolly creatures with drunken stagger,
Morphing next, into bleating, galloping joy.
Male feathered dinosaurs, strutting, and boasting their finery.
Females averting, glancing sideways, looking for perfect form.
Taking to the wing, playing the game of love and survival.
Males follow on, feeling the urgency of proliferation.
Warm sunny days, easing joints and lightening hearts.
Dreams of lazy days to come, of lemonade fizz,
Of strawberries red and candy coloured skirts.
Would it were that these days never ending be.

The Futures? You Chose!

'Tis the morn, a dawn of a new age born,
An age without prejudice, hate or scorn,
The age for friendship, for science of care.
A time to be green, a time to beware.
Let’s look to the future and never turn back,
Accepting our differences, for that's a ruinous track!
Shall we live for tomorrow in faith and in hope?
Climbing life's mountain, a slippery slope!
The hungry, the needy, no longer found.
The meek at last heard, from evil, no sound.
If this dream sounds impossible, just take note and trust,
For our planet to survive, fulfil it we must!

‘Tis the night, the night of an age dying,
Killed by the treachery, killed by the lying!
The age of hate, the science of war,
Into frail bodies’ black, white, yellow it tore!
The pain and the suffering, in endless torment
The politicians, our mentors? The rockets they sent.
The talks, the deceit, the torturing the crime,
The death of our 'mother' will take only time!
The devil looks on, his face filled with mirth,
The angel of death reaps the souls of the Earth

What a Load of Rubbish!

My mobile rang,"Hi Nev!" I said cheerily, "How's it going?"
Neville and I have been friends for years. I would always help him out and he me. That though, usually works out about 60/40 in his favour. Not that I'm concerned, you understand. That's just friendship, yes? Anyway, seeing as how he had rung me, I asked him, "What do you want doing?"
He just laughed. "I could do with an old bed dumping. It's a double bed but it will go on the top of the van."
Now my van was once his van, and he has the tendency, even though he sold it to his brother, in between me acquiring it, to call it the van, rather than your van. Which just makes me smile to myself.
"Ok no prob's!" I chirped, "See you in what? Ten minutes?" Now I also know Nev's ten minutes are more like twenty. To give you an idea, terms like 'just nip me here', usually means, two or three trips on the same journey.
After much planning on Nev's side, we eventually got the bulk of the bed strapped securely to the top of the van. The Bed heads we slung in the back.
"Right, are we taking it to the public tip at Ferrybridge, or the one at Castleford?" I asked.
"I think that Ferrybridge is slightly nearer" he decided
Off we went, bed on top of my little Astra van, although it looked quite weird, it was well fastened on, safe and secure. The 'ratchet type' nylon straps I had were ideal. Except that two of them didn't get much use, and so, were a pain to undo. This proved the case when we arrived at the Tip. We reversed up to the skip in the yard, and proceeded to try to undo the straps. As I have explained two were fine. But the other two were causing some consternation.
"'Scuse me! What do you think you're doing?" said an officious

voice.
“We’re having difficulty with these straps” I said, “I don’t suppose you have any freeing oil, do you?” I enquired
“No! I mean what are you doing with that thing?” He said pointing at the van
“We’re not dumping the van!” I said in mock alarm, trying to look hurt at the suggestion. All attempts at levity by me, seemed futile from the off.
“Very funny! [Although clearly not] Didn’t you read the notice?” Obviously a superfluous question. “Afraid not, missing your meaning!”
“You can’t tip here using a van!” He exclaimed, sounding as if I had committed a cardinal sin. “Come with me!”
With which he led us, by the ear lobe [jokin’], to the white notice. It was in letters so small, that it would make a loan agreement proud. It stated that commercial vehicles had to be accompanied by a ‘tipping certificate’. Or something along those lines.
“It’s okay! It’s not commercial rubbish. I’m just helping my friend out here, it’s his old bed, and he only has a saloon car.”
“You need to get registered!” he stated
“Yes, no problem, I will next time, Officer” I said trying to boost his ego. Unfortunately, we had a ‘Jobsworth’ here.
“Not so fast matey!” I hate matey, by the way, mate and buddy are fine, but there’s something about ‘matey’.
“You will have to get this thing registered, before you can tip here!”
At this point Nev interjected. “It’s really my fault buddy, it’s my bed. If you look closely, you will be able to see my imprint on the mattress. He’s just doing me a favour.” He said, trying to add some humour to the situation.
“Fact remains, you’re gonna have to go through to Denby Dale Road Tip, Wakefield, to register your vehicle, and get the paperwork. They’ll issue you with slips.” He stated adamantly.
“I don’t believe this!” I exclaimed, “You’re joking surely?” I took one

look at his officious little face and knew, jokes were off the menu!
"It's about a sixteen mile round trip to Denby Dale!" I said, after we had strapped the bed back on top of the van.
"I know!" said Nev, "Let's try Castleford!"
"Genius!" I replied, "That's only a ten mile round trip." I said, enthused
So off we set for the Castleford Tip. As we approached the gates, there were men on the gate. They were sitting in the gate house. As we drove up, two burly men in day glow yellow coats, waved us down.
"You can't come in here unless you have dockets." They stated
"But it's only domestic rubbish!" I almost cried in exasperation.
"Makes no nevermind, you need a docket!" He said with an almost [I swear!] evil grin.
"I don't believe this!" I shouted, as I turned to Nev. "They knew we were coming. Some sort of 'Commercial dumper alert' system"
"You're getting paranoid" said Nev, as ever the pragmatist.

"Wakefield!" I shouted, with gritty determination.
As we pulled into Denby Dale waste site, arms were waved furiously, and men in day glow yellow coats jumped out in front of us. Demanding we either stop, or die! Not really, but along those lines. We explained that we had come, in peace, seeking the god of dockets, and were allowed to park up. Adjacent to the 'docket obtaining office'.
I approached the window. She was a pretty little girl. Obviously fresh out of college, two CSE's and a desire to under achieve.
"Yeah?" she asked in a professional way, "Can I 'elp?"
"I do hope so!" I began hopefully, "I need 'the dockets' of the Great God Dumpingness!"
I lie, I said, "Could I please obtain the dockets, which I need to allow me to dump waste from a commercial vehicle, please!"
She replied, "Yeh, I need your Vehicle registration document, and a

Utility bill please"
"WOT!!!" I exploded, "I wasn't told that at Ferrybridge waste depot!"
"Well they should have!" She said helpfully
"I have my driver's license and a bill of sale for a refrigerator, plus my van's parked there!" I exclaimed
"Must be your registration document, plus a utility bill!" she replied
At this point, I said something that I must refrain from putting down on paper.
"Leave it!" said Nev, "I'll get rid of it somehow."
"NO!" I said, my mind now firmly set. "We'll leave the mattress here, and go for the documentation, come back get sorted and then dump it" I said
We proceeded to unstrap the bed,
"What you think you're doin'?" Came a voice from the ether.
We immediately strapped the bed back on. "Elvis has left the building!" I shouted, as we drove off, back to my house in Pontefract, to get the relevant documents. It was now rush hour of course!
We returned:
As I approached the window, I could see a change of receptionist.
"Hi there!" She quipped, "Can I help you?"
"I do hope so!" I almost pleaded, " I need the dockets for commercial vehicle dumping, please"
"Certainly!" she answered, "Is that the vehicle?" she enquired
"Yes" I said."Well I need some kind of I.D., a driver's license, or passport and your registration number"
"Don't you want the registration docu.....?" I stopped myself, "Here you are" I said exasperated once more. I gave her the relevant details.
"Thank you!" she said as she proceeded to print off the dockets.
I nearly kissed her, several times. In my mind at least.
"Let's unload the bed" said Nev
"NO!" I cried

As I drove into the depot at Ferrybridge, I had a smile which almost split my face in two!

Jenny

Jenny shivered in the rain, her head inside out.
The last one had punched her as she let out a shout,
“Be quiet! Or I’ll hurt you!” She’d backed off in alarm
He’d grabbed her roughly, badly twisting her arm
She’d fought back the tears, knowing this would show weakness,
Knowing full well if spotted, his attack then increases.
Jenny’d complied with his wishes, and in her mouth, she’d taken it.
Terrified now, her instincts telling her, ‘don’t seem it’.
When he’d ‘finished’, he’d just struck her again and again.
Her adrenalin soaked body, had not felt any pain.
Her survival was utmost, she was alive at least.
She had ridden out the horrors handed out by this Beast.
Jenny had remembered lessons the others had told.
“You’ve got to be careful, when a prostitute and just fifteen years old!”
She’d wiped herself down and tidying herself, returned to her corner.
The best spot on the street, just outside Sally’s Sauna.
She must score soon or suffer, a punter was needed.
But for once desperation took over, she forgot and hadn’t heeded,
All the things she’d been taught by her Mentors who knew.
She didn’t stand a chance, when it came, like a bolt from the blue.
“Check his eyes and his manner; make sure he’s not high!”
He seemed friendly enough this pleasant charming guy.
She’d looked at the ‘money’, of it he had reeked.
“A little pleasant company” was all that he seeked.
This time she would get paid, of that she was sure.
And later tonight she’d be pumping, Heroine pure.
Down the alley they went, he insisted, inside a shed,
She’d felt not a thing, throat cut, as to her death she’d bled.
Sally shivered in the rain, sixteen, her head inside out,
Off she had stormed, ringing in her ears, her Father’s angry shout.
That bastard would no longer touch her, in the way he did.
She would make her own way, no longer heeding, get rid.
The last one had hit her, and caused her great pain.

Sally thought she'd heard a whisper, as she stood in the rain,
"Get away Sally! My God if only you knew!"
"Death is approaching, tonight he comes for you!"
Alice shivered in the rain, fifteen, her head inside out.
Daddy had made her promise, what not to tell about.

The Time Is Near

When I look at all the hurt and anger in the world. I sometimes despair.
All the lies and deceit, in the name of religion and justice,
Which become unjust in themselves.
Evil is as a red hot poker, you can see it,
Sometimes you can feel it near, you are not able to grasp it!
Love is a fluid thing, it flows from person to person,
Like a river, It will gather momentum.
Until at the very end a calm gentle flow remains
As with water, grip your hands tightly,
Try to keep it for yourself, nothing but drops remain.
Hold it gently and let it trickle out, you will always be left with plenty.
We must all learn to love and accept love,
For if we do not we will be lost forever.
The time is oh so much closer than we realise.

Pleiades Pilgrims

One day some strangers passed by this way,
They took stock of our planet, and laid down our DNA.
Then headed back to Pleiades, promising, one day, they'd return.
Leaving us to our own devices, to grow and to learn.
Watching from afar, and pledging no interference
We started to learn, in the first instance.
Respecting our surroundings, the trees and the plants.
Also the animals, from the whales to the ants.
Then along came the industries, a desire to progress.
Mountains of refuse, creating a disgusting huge mess.
The waste became phenomenal, just a disgrace.
We've realised too late, with shame on our face.
That we've raped the earth, plundering our mother,
And stand toe to toe now, blaming each other.
We now have to face it, for out of time we have run.
As we move through the plane, our enemy is the Sun.
Time waits for no one, and the ages have past.
The flares are upon us, we expect the big blast.
If by chance we survive, for it's not something we've earned.
Not realised the consequences, not anything we've learned.
Should the volcanoes die down, and flooding abate.
Could we all learn to love, instead of pure hate?
Cast out the money mongers, who seek, obeyance and control.
Build a charter of peace, and would everyone enrol?
I hope so, but fear, not, for there's so many who are blind.
They care just for themselves, and not for mankind.
Looking up to the stars, I let my mind wander.
Our family from the Pleiades, will they return I ponder.
With hope in my heart, I dream of the outcome we crave,
For our brothers and sisters to return and our souls to save.

Alone

He looked around him, the photographs, the music, his life.
They seemed meaningless somehow, his head filled with strife.
He thought of the things that he'd done the good deeds and bad.
Remembering the help he'd given, in times of need, made him sad.
The promises they gave, the thanks, then let downs and betrayals.
He not wanting monetary reward, just the truth not denials.
They had taken so much from him, his life, night and day.
He'd been there for them all, knowing exactly what to say.
Now today, alone he stood, looking around at his lot.
No wife there to greet him, no happy kids had he got.
The one bedroom apartment, sounding hollow and cold.
She'd packaged up their life, taken off, house was sold.
"There's always someone else, we don't have a life,
I want a separation, I need space!" Said his wife.
He'd, gone on a bender, twice waking up in the gutters.
Turned off his phone, needing time, put up shutters.
Time heals they say, but believe, it leaves your soul with a scar.
Distance doesn't make a heart grow fonder; often it's a bridge too far.
Mustering strength from deep within, he pulled back from the abyss.
Vowing to collect his life together, because them all he did miss.
Then a knock on his door, steeling himself, he wouldn't send them away.
Opening it, he smiled, saying, "Hello, I'll be your councillor today"

The Watcher [2]

I hate these cold mornings! Coping with the dirty, icy slush that splashes around me. “Hey watch it Moron!!!” Some people, they get in their cosy warm cars, and don’t give a damn for the rest of us out here in the elements. They drive along with total disregard, for who they’re splashing!

Lookout here comes ‘Humpty coffee guy’! He’s a bit sad I suppose, hung over from the night before, careering along, spilling coffee over everyone and bumping into them without apologising! He goes into that bar over the way there, Sam’s. He was talking to me last night. He had staggered out, well more like thrown out actually, as it was closing time. He must have spotted me, and so he stumbled over to greet me! He needed supporting. What he poured out to me, from the depths of his soul was heart wrenching. I must admit it brought tears to my eyes. His wife had been killed in a car accident along with his two babies, John three, and Alice, barely one year old. The sad thing was it was his fault, the booze you see! He’d had over the limit. It wasn’t entirely his fault they’d been at an engagement party; he’d been driving, had refused most of the night, then succumbed. Thinking one or two won’t hurt now! But he might have reacted more quickly and avoided the truck driver, who had done too many hours and had fallen asleep at the wheel. He had been in pieces since poor guy, taking the full blame on his shoulders. So there he was holding onto me for grim death, crying bitter tears of remorse, and saying how he needed to die, and join them. The bar owner, Sam probably, had presumably called the cops, because they had come to my rescue, but not before he had spewed up all over me. Gosh that stunk!

Anyway here he comes right on cue, acting out his pain filled day. “Hey watch it fella!” a few including me cried, as he spilt hot coffee over us. Poor guy, guess no one knows or cares except me.

Look who’s coming now! Like clockwork she rushes here every morning, always on time, to this same spot where I stand. I just pretend to get on with my job, but really I watch and listen. Here he comes now, late as usual! Yes, here come the excuses, yes, and the underground, bad connection. Always the same! Now here comes the slobbering, get a room!! Anyone would think that they hadn’t seen each other for months, let alone yesterday. But I know the secret! I get to see all sorts of things while doing my job. He’s married! Cheating on his wife, I’ve seen them going into the café opposite at lunch time, with the kids, sometimes. You can tell, peck on the cheek greeting and when they leave to go their separate ways, he gives her an occasional full one on the lips, for reassurance. The Slime ball! Lovely kids they are, they call him daddy with such affection, and she looks so happy, and so beautiful! The ‘grass is always greener’, they say, no it isn’t, I say! Idiot!

Oh no, it’s Mad Joe! He’s a Bum! He ties his dog up, and always asks me to look after it for him. Scruff’s a friendly chap, tail going like a rotor blade all the time. Loads of passers by pat him, and say hello to the little guy. But he’s covered in fleas at the moment and... “Hey Scruff! No!!” God he’s just peed down me. Where the hell’s Joe? He’s off begging food and cigarettes from the commuters and surrounding café’s etc. Thank goodness here he comes now! “Where yah been Joe, have you seen what Scruff’s done? He's peed on me!" Joe just grunted untying the dog and shuffled off muttering.

"Gee thanks! Call again!"

Yes I see all sorts when I'm doing my job. Think maybe I'll write a book one day.

"Watch out!!" Did you see that? A young woman just leapt out in front of that bus! Oh my God, what a mess! Surely she's dead? People are crowding around her, kneeling down. I can just make her out over the top of them. It's Mary for Christ's sake! Oh no poor Mary! She's a prostitute. Make that **was** a prostitute, now, I think. Poor Mary! She's stood with me many times, emptying out her soul. Saying how she was 'going to get straight', and get out of the game. That all she needed was a chance, poor kid! She told me she had been abused as a child, left home at thirteen. Yes you heard right, thirteen! For Christ's sake! What a life, on the streets selling your body to any animal, shooting up, and getting beat up for your troubles! I could weep with pity!

She was dead they took her away in a body bag, barely sixteen. What a waste! The bus driver is distraught poor fella! He sat next to me, and we wrapped him in a blanket, someone gave to Officer Riley. Now he'll be upset! Officer Riley I mean. He's your typical friendly cop, Irish of course, suppose you guessed by the name? He's often stood with Mary and me on dark cold nights, and given her his cape to warm her through for a while. The hours he's spent, trying to get her on this or that programme, to no real satisfactory end result. He'd always remained friendly towards her, trying to ease her out of her situation, rather than bullying her into submission. This as we know, would have resulted in her moving into darker recesses, and more trouble. No trouble now though for sad Mary!

Officer Riley has gotten the traffic moving again, and they sent a relief driver for the bus, poor chap, the driver I mean.

What a day it's been and my shift hasn't really started yet.

"Hey come on!" Kids! That ball hit me then! What with balls, dogs and whatever else, I'll be glad when it quietens down.

Here comes Jimmy the newspaper vendor. What's he yelling? 'Man commits suicide, jumps off bridge!" Wonder who that is? The cheek of it he's leaned the poster up against me. "Oi!!" I can't quite see who it is! I wonder who? It's getting dark; I'll put my light on and see whether I can make the suicide chap out. Oh my God! It's Mr Wilson I think! The guy from the bar, the guy who threw up on me last night! It must have got too much for him. Poor Mr Wilson!

Told you, what a day! I tell you, I'm glad I'm just a lowly CCTV camera!

A Perfect Form

I stopped and stooped the other day,
I don't know why, I'm sorry I just can't say!
I held a daisy in my hand; it looked so small and fragile,
And then, as if not seen before, it did beguile
Me with its beauty. As I looked and did behold,
Perfect form and symmetry coloured white and gold.
I held it for an age and could not let go.
Its wonderment filled my soul, flooding me so,
With tears. I just cannot explain the joys I felt,
I beheld its wondrous beauty, as I dwelt,
This perfect almost secret form, unseen by the daily eye.
Given not a second thought, as humans passed it by.
Please take advice, if you would, you will prosper, tarry a while.
Cup carefully your hand, around bloom and leaf, believe, you will smile,
Or shed a tear or two.

The Guest

Come! Sit here beside me and tarry a while,
For as you know I'm lonely, I'm lost in a style
Of a time I no longer know or care for. A time
hanging in a fog of remorse, blanketed with a lime
of burning lies and deceit. Your honesty holds me in awe
and in trust. Of your future? I look and thought I saw,
A glimmer of hope. And retribution to those false, smiling
eyes. Satiating our minds with promises false. Lucifer's beguiling
ways. Reveal once again your ideas, so devastating to those
of closed mind. To those who seek naught but to strike blows
at the weak and the poor. Tell me of your terrible plans,
To strike them from existence, to drive them from our lands.
This plan, not of missiles and warheads. But of staff and of dove.
Of nothing more than a world wrapped with love.
Tell me this and once more I will sleep.
Down here in my bed, your secret to keep
between us two, 'til the moment arrives. When,
I will meet you once more my friend, be with you again.

The Politician

Sally sits alone in her 4x8 room, her baby on her lap,
Billy sits in the doorway cold and alone, a destitute chap.
It happened so fast! The bailiffs they came,
Men in black, men without shame.
The gas the electric, the food bills the rent,
No food in the cupboards, on loan sharks it's spent.
It happened so fast! The arguments the blows,
How did it happen? God only knows.
The first ones ignored, the next, angry in red,
The official ones, cower down, just stay in bed!
“Who cares? We should for each other!”
"I'm the one for you, my brother!"
"Vote for me I'll put things right!"
“Justice for you, I'll fight with my might!"
“This government, I’ll get on the right road”
The politician slides into his second abode,
"It's cold out there let's turn up the heat!"
"I'll look in the fridge and see if there's meat!"
“These expenses they go nowhere at all!"
Grabbing the phone, gives Luiggi's a call,
"No send it! It’s freezing out there!"
On a carpet threadbare,
Sally weeps alone with her baby,
Billy, alive tomorrow? Maybe!
Who cares?

The Secret

No! Cast your mind onto the sea of future.
Set sail for unknown ports, across life's oceans.
Be not afraid of what's left behind! Face the beast Present.
Listen carefully, to hear the secret, the secret sought by many,
The secret captured by few.
The way is strewn with the souls of 'turned' men.
Falter not, across the abyss of failure, for to fail, is but to start again!
And to start again, is to live! To fail and turn, is to die,
To die in a state of eternal limbo, without knowing.
And when you cross swords with, 'if only', or 'but', strike them down!
For they are your enemies! They plant the seeds of doubt, in fragile minds.
Gird your armour, built of faith and hope and past failings.
Take up your lance of knowledge and mount your steed, Endeavour.
Ride forth across the plains of adventure,
Stop for no man!
Stop for no thing!
Live this way and you may truly live!

This Hamlet

This abode, this Hamlet of careless ignorant men,
Not ours but taken, greedily in both hands,
No tear, drops upon the bleeding earth,
Pain unheard as heart and bowels are torn asunder.
We toil away to slake a thirst with disregard.
Warful man, insentient, with uncompromising hate.
Brother killing brother, in religious cause.
Trundling forth, the sap weeps away.
A silent scream unnoticed.
Not of fear, but consternation.
Others look on and shake their weary heads.
This Hamlet will soon sleepy be.
Will lay its head and with a sigh recover
Its weary bones stroked by time.
As it casts off our dead unwanted husks.
The age for care, lost in ages unremembered.
We regard ourselves so significant,
And so are lost.

"It has come to our notice that you have been..... Shall we say? Bending the rules of engagement!" said the Grand Overseer.

"All I've been doing is using another, might I say? Tried and tested method!" Objected Collector 106

"You know all too well the rules!" Interjected Prime collector 10,"We do not collect close to open habitats, for obvious reasons."

"All well and good Sir" said 106 to the Overseer, "but surely the cat's out of the bag, so to speak, already, is it not? So do we not need to step up our operations before they work things out?"

"On the contrary, we need to pick the units more carefully. Selecting them for their availability. Do you understand what that means, 106?" said the Prime collector.

"Yes, I know the Directive, I'm not stupid. I must be one of your top Collectors?" He wailed.

"More can sometimes be less 106, and collecting which causes more than a raised eyebrow of concern, only serves to make it harder for the others. They have a job to do as well, and you could jeopardise their living. In fact all of our lives." Said the Prime

"I really think you're over reacting!" snarled 106, "I don't think that it will make any significant difference. Sure! For a day or two they might show some real concern. But in my experience, in hindsight, maybe not even a day. Then they will return to their mortgages and school fees and all the other distractions which keep them focussed and afraid. Not the fact that So and So's disappeared without any word, from number eighteen. Surely that's why we picked them in the first place? The way in which their society's changed, the indifference, the breakdown in communities."

"Yes, but if we take too many, too quickly, they may begin to wake up. They may begin to notice and start questioning. Replied the Prime Collector.

"Well how about starting a war, or at least helping one along? The misdirection trick! There is a conflict in their middle East. We could take out a President. They would all blame one another, and the war would start. We could have a field day!"

"That is a backup plan" said the Overseer, "meanwhile you are to adhere to the regulations. Only select the ones which have fallen by the wayside, rejected by their society. Is that clear, 106?"

"Yes Sir!" Scowled 106 "Perfectly plain"

"And remember the basics, don't get them scared or worried. Use the sedation beam, if necessary" said Prime Collector.

"But that involves a two man team sir!" cried 106, "and it also halves my credits!"

"Yes but you'll also collect twice as many, even maybe more, and he may also, maybe, keep you out of trouble"

"Sir!" 106 left muttering to himself.

"We may have trouble with that boy" said the Overseer.

"No maybe about it!" replied the Prime, "Still he's a top collector, and we desperately need them as you know."

"Yes, indeed." Said the overseer thoughtfully rubbing his chin.

“I don’t care what they say, all I seem to do these days is work. We’ll collect as many as we can, as quickly as we can. If we leave abused kids alone and stay away from old people’s homes, and the obvious ones. We could manage say one hundred a day between us. That’s seventy for me and thirty for you” said 106.

“What!” cried out 2010, “that’s unfair; I’ll be doing the same work as you, perhaps all the heavy work, if I know you.”

“Yes but I’m more senior, and I’ve put in the intelligence work” he smirked.

“He’ll do” said 106

“What the drunk?” said 2010, “they stink the transporter out!”

“Doesn’t matter, we don’t have to stand the cost of the sedation cartridges. He’s already sedated”

As they lifted victim number one hundred and one into the transporter, 2010 said, “Why do we have to sedate them anyway, it seems a waste?”

“Don’t they teach you anything at Collectors school anymore?” sneered 101 “The adrenalin gets into the blood and spoils the flavour.”

“Oh! So if they’re knocked out, it has the same effect, no adrenalin rush?”

“Well! Who’s a clever little collector then?” jeered 106. “I make the count one hundred and one, okay?”

“Yes fine” said 2010, smiling.

“You’ve been a busy boy, one hundred and two altogether!” said the Tallyman, “Any difficult ones?”

“No not really, the last one was the easiest really!” said 2010, he must inform the Overseer, he thought, with a satisfied smile.

Websu

Your Washed clothes look dingy, they're really not right.

Just leave it to us though; we'll bring them up bright.

They're covered with old stains it's a Bio you need,

If you don't get all those out, then, they'll go to seed.

If you knew what was on them, then Zudzo's no good,

They're riddled with bacteria and germs not understood.

Our products built to cure it, stop worrying right now.

It kills disease from the Chicken, the Swine and the Cow.

We don't want you stressing and freaking yourself out.

Our powders the only one for you, none comes near it about.

It's a little bit dearer, but we think you'll agree.

That, WEBSU, what you don't understand, is clearly for you! You see?

Please note: weBSu is an accepted & registered Trademark

The Grey Man

He sits in the corner, or stands, wears a slight swagger.
An invisible man, a grey man. Not a ten pint bragger.
He smiles quite politely at everyone's jokes.
He sits by himself, outside were he smokes.
He's no Brad Pitt and he's not some other superstar.
But if you look at him closely there's ' je ne sais qua'
He dresses quite smartly in suits not in jeans.
He could be a man of incredible means!
No one will know though, no one will ask.
Moving without complaint, when pushed. Not a task.
He sips down his lager then brandy, perhaps gin.
A haze on his face, with a lopsided grin.
The barman shouts "Time please!" As he empties the trays.
The grey man in stupor, blurred thoughts of better days.
Staggers out of the doorway and off down the street.
Down towards home and whatever to meet.
He reaches his castle, his safe sanctuary.
And he opens his fridge, no food, "I know pantry!"
There's nothing in there though, at least nothing to eat.
Maybe some crackers or tinned processed meat.
"Now just wait a moment what's this I espy?"
He lifts out the bottle with a jubilant cry.
"I'd forgotten about you my dearest best friend.
How could I ere forget you? When you help me no end."
He pours out the whiskey he'd bought just that eve.
A promise when buying it "'until Christmas I'll leave!"
"I'll just have a stiffener. A nightcap or two"
"What's that? Who's talking? What's it got to do with you?"
He empties the bottle, slips into the dark, makes a terrible racket.
Hitting his head, splitting his nose. Tearing his shirt and spewing on his jacket.
"I wonder what his name is? He's been laid here some time!
No sign of a family. No sign of a break in, nor crime.
He's lived all alone here, you can tell by the mess.

Had a bad drink problem, by the bottles I'd guess!
Dressed rather sharply though. Kept himself clean.
No valuables or trinkets or luxury goods to be seen."
"Ah well! Bag 'im 'n' tag 'im, John Doe, if you would?"
"Why they get in this state, I've never understood!"
Off drove the officials without a second thought on their mind.
As to what kind of life he had. Was he mean? Was he kind?
Just another body count another 'Joe', on the slab.
Another statistic, another headline in a local Tab.
He sits in the corner, or stands, wears a slight swagger.
A grey man, an invisible man. Not a ten pint bragger.
If you turn around slowly and look to your right.
Take it easy and heed me, for you may get a fright!
Carefully look in the mirror, and what do you see
Now what colour suit is that, Grey man? Tell me!

Solar Storm

I don't advocate anarchy, neither do I concur with crimes.
But what do you do when the reality is; it's the end of our times?
Supplies and food the Juggernaut, no longer for ages, delivers.
All types of fuel turned off, so everyone sits and shivers.
The Government's lies uncovered and debunked.
Engine Management systems failed, burnt and defunked.
All Microchips useless and to a crisp fried.
Bank vaults on 'shutdown', with all the cash and 'valuables' inside.
Vehicles and machines stand idle and useless.
Once a sign of wealth the 'Rolls', no longer any use to us.
Cash, diamonds and gold, no good as tender, indeed
The only tradable currency now, just food and seed
Ordinary people once neighbour and brother,
Sated with greed and survival, turn on each other.
The dogs roam in packs, baying for a kill.
An old woman in the street, begging and losing the will.
The pack sense her weakness and surrounding leap forward.
As she's torn to the ground, a bony hand reaches skyward.
"God, please have pity", she begs one last time.
But of her God and her saviour she sees not a styme.
Babies are crying, their howls are of hunger.
Anxious parents in desperation anticipate murder.
No more food in the cupboards, none on supermarket shelves.
As people fight for every last morsel, for themselves.
Authority non-existent now as Law and order wanes.
One weak man's losses are another stronger man's gains.
As the former fall by the wayside, no one seems to care.
The populace hurry past or just stand and stare,
Waiting for a chance to search his dead body.
Tearing at his clothes, well worn and now shoddy.
He pleads to them for help, "Please show me mercy!"
"It's not personal, just survival!" they tell him tersely.
I remember the first days it happened, so well.
But the first thing to break down I could not tell.
Cars in the street were slowing to a halt.

Heavy trucks, now without servos, crashing with a jolt.
What was worse, planes plummeting out of the skies.
The air was filled with horrible screeching and cries.
Carnage continued as ships could not stop.
Helicopters facing a two hundred foot drop.
Grabbing my mobile to phone the police for aid.
It was dead as a doornail, as I watched it's screen fade.
I turned on the telly to see what was happening out there.
Nothing at all stirring, as it gave back a blank stare.
Confused and upset, I next turned the radio on.
Once again silence, where had the world at large gone?
It's nearly two months now, but it seems like an age,
As I glance over my shoulder trying the distance to gauge.
The distance from the 'hunters', as I am now their prey.
I need to put mileage between us, while it is still yet day.
I'll find a forest nice and thick, there to erect my tent.
Somewhere to rest and wonder why this plague was sent.
At last I've found a haven, deep inside the wood.
Trying to stay awake and listen, but find that it's no good.
The noises have awoken me, and I try to rouse my mind.
Half asleep, I scramble around, my makeshift spear to find.
My eyes are open now and the last thing that I see,
Is the deadly point of my own spear, reigning down on me.

Ode to an Ovine

Torrid times in torrid towns with torrid people scuttling by.
"You must fear this, you must fear that", wringing hands, anxiety, fit to cry.
Pushing in, pushing out, "Damn the queues!" and Ovine stares,
Waiting for trains, waiting for buses, lining up in perfect pairs.
Watching the clock, watching the watch, precious seconds flying past.
Words of anger said in temper, reaching the 'office desk' at last.
Count the numbers in the columns, making all the figures fit.
Force the square peg in the round hole, carrying on with determined grit.
Responsibility is the order, firmly on your shoulders sat,
When walls collapse, come tumbling down, that's where it's squarely at.
Swallowing burgers, fish paste sarnies, Bio-yoghurts by the tub.
Chicken nuggets, crisps 'n' nibbles, the Microwave a vital hub.
Back once more nose to grindstone, selling just one more mobile phone,
Sitting back 'taking a second', listening in to the incessant drone.
Close the deal, end the chapter, hammer in the final nail.
Hooter sounded, homeward headed, pace now of the proverbial snail.
Grab some tea, turn on the telly, fall asleep while watching dross.
Dreams of lambs in flowery meadows? No, just the face of an angry boss.
Slumbering deeply, alarm is ringing, turning it off in disbelief.
Missing breakfast, through the door, "Yet another day of grief!"

The thing in the corner

There's something quite mysterious in the corner of my room.
It doesn't bark or chirp or meow and it doesn't go vroom,
I've tried to stay away from it, but no matter how I try,
It always seems to pull me in and tries to catch my eye.
Sitting down upon my couch I'll try it to ignore.
But every time I do this it calls to me more and more.
Why can't it seem to let me be, as I try to do my work.
It seems to want to stop me and tries to make me shirk.
I've tried making it face the wall but it seems there's no effect.
I've even put it on my New Year's list, of things I must reject.
Why does it rear its ugly head when I just want to study.
It must think that I am a friend, or even its best buddy.
When left alone it shrieks at me, it really is quite loud.
But now I've learned to turn my cheek, I really am quite proud!
It's a while now since I noticed it, almost forgetting it's there.
Almost gotten to a point where its presence I can bare!
It's got a spider for a friend, with cobwebs strewn across.
I knew it would settle down as soon as it discovered who's boss.
There's a gentle tap, tap on my keyboard, instead of a melee.
But one thing is for sure, I won't be turning on that telly!!

A Place of Souls

I gazed the night sky, washed with dead blood,
Alight, sprinkled with gleaming souls of futures past.
Espying a soul returning, as it streaked in from the East
Its joy was plain for all to see, as a trail of glee it left.
Wishing I could be there, as born once more it was.
Screaming joy and will to live, to start again once more.
Another streaked in from the west, staying me with awe.
But my journey called me to carry on, delay was not a choice.
I had to reach the place of souls, so travel on I must.
I remember the bullet as it struck, the pain I don't recall.
I'd left my daughter in the car, what would become of her?
"Daddy bring me back some sweets, if you would be so kind"
I'd looked and smiled a knowing smile, back at her eager face.
I remember his desperate look, as the tiller refused him blank
Turning round in panic, he levelled the gun at me.
It wasn't hate; it wasn't greed, but needing one more fix.
Bang went the gun, I looked in shock, as the light faded away.
I must get on, I must journey there, this I know as fact
I don't know how I know it, but it tugs at me within.
I'm so sorry God if you exist, for any pain I've caused.
But if you're there protect my child and keep her safe
She was all that was dear to me, please keep her by your side.
I love her so; it has no bounds, as all with child will know
I saw another from the South gliding in to land.
Then I felt a presence close to me, I swore it was a hand.
A voice so gentle flooded over me, it filled me with such warmth,
"Not yet my friend you cannot go, your time here is not finished."
I felt a hand wrapped around mine then, light flooding in my eyes.
"Oh Daddy dear I love you so, I thought you'd left me here!"

Acid Tears

As I walk midst the rustling leaves dressed now in garbs
Of reds browns and golds. Regal and ready for sleep,
In those coming inclement days of Jack's desire.
Ready to stand the forthcoming trial, with strength and dignity.
A trial not of manly origin, but of ancient significant things.
Our mother turns once again, looking on with sadness at her children.
Their wicked stupid ways, leaving her with tears of acid.
Slowly killing her oldest children,
The ones who support her, so she may give life.
The ones who fill our lungs with a precious gift.
We care not for these gifts, given, but not freely!
There is a price!
Our understanding, our love and our care, or else if we do not
At our peril. No more a second chance and third and more.
Too late it will shortly be, for our mother now turns from us.
And we now have to face our just rewards.
The rewards for lies, broken promises, a hundred fold.
Our mother looks back and cries in despair

Just Press...

'Please continue to use your keypad to answer the following question. This will help us to deal with your enquiry as quickly as possible. For Mobile phone enquiries, press 1; For Broadband enquiries, press 2; For all other enquiries, press 3. For Broadband contract enquiries press1; For broadband pay as you go enquiries press 2;....................For "is there still anybody there?" Enquiries, press 99;.................For, 'if by now you're suicidal and don't know which method to use', enquiries, press Zero.'

You all know how it goes, you've been there, and then you get through to a call centre somewhere in the Jungles of Borneo. Don't get me wrong! These poor people are only trying to make a pittance to survive, and it's not their fault. I've spent many hours cogitating this puzzle, who is to blame? I always seem to come up with the same answer. **We are!** Because we have created a culture where we are all terrified, of being without our mobile phones and out of touch. Although whatever went wrong with calling round to see someone and chatting to them face to face? I don't know, do you? Anyway back to the call. "Is this the number you are calling about?" [in pigeon English]
"No it's about my mobile broadba...."

"Please to give me the number that you call about"
"0700000000.. " I give the number. He repeats it and gets two digits wrong.
"No it's 0700000000.."
"Thankyou what is your enquiry?"
"I havc had a problem trying to top up my pay-as-go broadband. I tried several times to…."
"Just a moment, please while I check this" Silence……………..
"What is your name…..What is your postcode…..What is your card number, which you used to top up?"
" It has topped up your account by £10.00 on that date Sir."
"I know that! But if you'll let me explain? It has also given me a message several times saying, 'this top up could not be completed at this time, please try again later'. Or something to that effect, and yet Three payments of £25.00, have disappeared from my bank account..Where please, has this money gone to?" At this point, I can feel the seasonal spirit of good will dissipating, rapidly.
"But the only amount you have topped up your account by is £10.00 sir"
I take a deep breath. "Yes but your system has also taken seventy five pounds from my bank account, and it's nowhere to be seen on my broadband account!"
"Just give me a minute, please sir" Silence for another five minutes or so.
"This is not our fault sir. I have just spoken to my supervisor and you will have to contact your bank to get this put right"
"So you are saying it's my banks fault?"
"Yes sir, most certainly"
"Right, if you're sure" I say with trepidation, "Thank you I will ring them then"
"Thank you sir, is there anything else I can help you with?"
"Well you haven't exactly…. No thanks, goodbye!" I hold myself back, with a sigh.

'For credit card enquiries, dial 1; For the Spanish inquisition dial 2; If you are a Muslim or a Jew, and wish to argue your case directly to the Pope, press 666; for all other options hold your breath for twenty minutes, if you are still alive by the time the holding music, 'Holst's Planets' have finished, we will cut you off and you can start again!'

".......So basically what you're saying is, that's it's the Mobile phone companies fault, Right?"
"Yes sir you need to ring them back, and get them to fax us a release on these funds, which have been authorised by you to go to them. Give them the authorisation codes which I have furnished you with."

'For a kick in the nuts, dial 999 first.......'
"....We do not know what these codes are sir. You must wait seven days to see whether the money is returned to you and if not you must kiss seventy five pounds goodbye"{not really the last bit, but I was about to scream}
"But all you have to do, is to fax a release to my bank at one of these numbers I can give you, and they will then release my money, back into my account!"
"Just one minute sir."

Ten minutes later, just as I was beginning to lose the will to live. "I am afraid..." my heart sunk beyond sight, "we do not have the facilities to do this sir, you...."

"Hang on! You do not have the facilities to fax, or did you mean faculties?"
"Sir?"
"Never mind, leave it with me. Thanks!"
"Thank you sir is there anything else I can do fo....?"

I missed the rest.

“Good afternoon sir. How may I help you ?” asked the bank clerk at the desk of my local branch.
I looked long and hard into his tender young eyes but resisted the temptation.
“It’s concerning seventy five pounds which appears to be hanging somewhere in the ether!” I said with a dry, twisted smile.

One hour later, taken up mainly, by the young man scurrying about, making enquiries and phone calls. “…….So what you have to do sir, is ring them up and ask them to fax us a release, and you should have the money back into your account. Possibly before you reach retirement age or die. Maybe!” [Aaaaghh!!!]
“Can you tell me, purely out of some weird, macabre fascination. Where my money is exactly? As it doesn’t show on my statement! Where’s it gone, just that it’s gone! And it doesn’t show on my Broadband statement, as having been received.”
“Yes sir it’s in ‘awaiting clearance’, waiting for the broadband service to collect it”
“Yes but the whole point **is!!!!** They have no intention of collecting it, and as it’s **my** money! Why in God’s name, can’t you put it back into my account?
“Because you’ve authorised them to take it, Mr Howard”
“But they don’t feckin want it!!!” I was now lost for reasonable words as you can probably imagine. “Look I’ll sign a release or whatever stating that ‘Ding-dong Telecomms’, don’t want the money and I authorise its recall” I was grasping at straws, and seeing my money fade into non existence.
“I can try that for you sir, but I can’t promise anything”
I wrote out, and signed the release, on paper he brought me.
“Right I’ll post that in the eternal (yes I did spell that correctly, as I’ve had dealings with internal mail, as well! That’s another story) mail

for you sir."
"Thank you" I almost managed
"Thank you sir. Is there anything el….."
I was out the door before he'd finished!

Feeling desperate and just needing to hear a friendly voice, I rang the Samaritans.
'For suicides, press 1; For Mental cruelty, press 2; For….'
I pressed 1, **hard!!!**

An Ancient Returns

From ages past, she returns.
Turning full circle across time and space.
Returning as promised not a saviour, or perhaps, hold!
She could yet bring the promise, the promise of spiritual change.
A chance to evolve, to cast off these mortal chains,
These chains, unwanted gifts, from unwanted 'Gods'.
False gods, who will cower in fear,
In their self made tombs of hypocrisy and lies

Forewarned

We were warned, our sightless eyes not looking,
Our deaf ears closed tightly shut, against the cries of fear.
The tortured 'mother' left raped and bleeding, life ebbing.
Her children, the innocents, dumb, unable to ask why?
Only lying in mother's arms, life's force leaving their crippled bodies.
They came, they saw! Their eyes were open.
They heard, their ears were ready to hear
The piteous cries of innocents. Their rage unleashed, bathed in disgust.
"Not our fault!" we all cried, "We weren't aware!"
They looked down upon us and passed their terrible judgment.
A year to repent. To open our eyes and hear the cries,
Mother just smiled, with a knowing smile
A smile bearing knowledge of centuries.
A year gone past and they returned.
They closed their ears, they looked away
Those piteous cries, those bleeding souls.
Onto mothers skirts we bled as essence waned.
We were warned our lifeless eyes no longer able to see.
We were warned our useless ears unable to hear
They went away and left our desperate souls to wonder, " Why?"

Highways of Time

Could you ride the Stallions of time?
Could you chase the Goblins of rhyme?
Catch the tail of the serpent of ages,
Fight the demons, surviving their rages!
If you succeed in this and still be able,
You may search the galaxy for fact and fable,
Finding the answers, your reward? Your purse?
To be, at last, as one, with the universe!

I Was Only Doing My Job

As I stood in the queue, it must have been some two dozen people long, I looked at the empty windows, and sighed unbelievingly. Why is it that, at what seems like peak time to me, do the people who serve on counters, usually where we queue to obtain money, take their breaks? They know we have to stay if we need our money; we don't have much choice in the matter, or is it just me going at the wrong time? It seems to me like every time I go! Or is it me being a moaning old fart again?

Anyway as I glanced around taking in the view, and studying the masses of forms on display V8's, V6's, EBGB's. Once again, is it just me, or do we seem to spend the best part of our waking hours just filling in forms? What happened to the *computer* age? I thought by now it would be a matter of just pushing a couple of buttons.

I then spotted something which made me chuckle, macabre but it did. It was a 'Last Will and Testament' form. I glanced at the queue ahead of me and wondered if I should get one and fill it in there and then, and get the shuffling old lady in front to witness it. As if she was reading my mind (I'm beginning to believe I'm a Telepath, or is that telepathetic?), she turned and smiled and nodding in the direction of the afore-said form, she said, "Wish my Bert had filled one of those things in, I had a right old time when he popped off and left me!"

Now at this point I knew I should not have engaged her, but seeing as the line didn't seem to be moving. I thought it may be a way of helping the time pass. I smiled and said, "Oh my! What happened then?" I got the old dear's complete life history. During this she looked at the large parcel under my arm and asked unnecessarily, if I was posting it. I almost replied no, and that I had just come in for the company, sparkling wit and conversation, but I couldn't hurt her feelings. She went on to explain that she was fed up with queuing every week, and that she came for her money at the same time, same day, and there was always a queue. I thankfully resisted the temptation to point out, that it may be prudent to come for it later in the day, or even the following day. I have found that the average Brit likes queuing, and moaning about it, seemingly obtaining a perverse enjoyment of some kind.

As we reached the head of the line, the 'by now grating on my nerve ends voice', came over the Tanoy, 'Position number six please!' The old dear turned to me and said once more unnecessarily, "You're next now dear!" But then added a tiny bit annoyingly, "D'you know? You could have gone straight to the parcel window with that large package? Bye Bye now dear!" I hung my head in despair.

'Position number two please!" I moved forwards to the window. "Can I post this please?" I said lifting the parcel up onto the shelf in front of the window.

"Have you queued with that? You could have gone straight to the parcels window!"

I just sighed.

"If you take it up there, I'll get someone to you"

I sighed again and moved to the Parcels window. Ten minutes later, "Are you the gent who queued, instead of waiting here?" the man said with a grin.

"Yes!" I replied with an icy smile. He took it through the window and after weighing it, and checking the address asked, "What's the value of it sir?"

"About forty pounds" I replied "Why?"

"Do you wish to insure it sir?"

"What for?" I asked

"In case of loss or damage sir!"

"It's only going to go to Leeds, and it's going to a Post Box number. Should it get lost over a journey of twelve miles, or will someone play football with it?" I exclaimed.

"There's no reason to take that attitude sir! I'm only doing my job!"

"I'm sorry!" I said "I'm tired, and a little irritated!" and trying to make amends, said "How much is the insured postage?" I nearly fainted; the insured postage was over twice the normal rate. "I don't think so young man; I'll take the normal rate thanks!"

I left the Post office shaking my head in disbelief and despair.

As I reached my van, and sat in the driver's seat, I glanced at the windscreen. There, as large as life, you guessed it, a parking ticket! I leapt out of the van, pulled off the ticket and read it. Three minutes late! Three minutes! I spotted the warden, or whatever they're calling them now, and approached him. "Couldn't you wait three minutes?!"I cried "I've had to queue in the Post Office!"

"I'm only doing my job sir! If you'll take my advice, next time you come to this Post Office, I'd come on another day, it's always full in there on this day. The old dears collect their pensions! Have a nice day now!"

I sighed, deep and long.

Moving On

Leaving my vessel I drift into oblivion,
Floating by lost souls and hopes,
Into eternal peace, solitude and space.
Flying free, umbilical chords cut,
Forever escaping this Human 'Race'.
My energy is free, set loose,
Untethered from its mortal coil.
Unhindered by ‘cant’s, mustn’t and don’ts
No longer restricted to earth’s terrestrial soil
My being bombarded by false knowledge
Realisation at last, as I sip the honey
A place neither of greed nor of hate
A place not of possessions nor money
A collective of love, of knowing.
Essences gathered, bound by true reality.
Irresistible, inarguable, indisputable truth
Far removed from the truth of ‘normality’
Ascended at last to a level where we belong.
A joining, yet separate, entwined and complete.
Travelling across time and distance of space.
At last no restrictions of rules to compete.
We pass through the cosmos, no distance too far.
Not needy of succour, no sustenance desired.
The boundaries of eternity no longer eluding.
At last becoming the light, to which we aspire.

Stop Them!

'Latch-key kids' left to their own devices, cruel intentions,
Parents with cruel indifference,
Looking the other way and blaming others.
Chasing that unobtainable pot of gold!
The true price?
A child with no honour or values.
Or worse in prison,
Or worse still, dead in the gutter!
'Blood', running free in the streets.

The Family

I had a wonderful dream last night,
I awoke to find that everything was alright.
Our extended family from the stars had returned.
And because of this all wars had adjourned.
They warned us of our follies and the ways we don't share.
Then they told us quite bluntly, that we must take care.
This was not a request and not to be taken lightly.
We were in trouble now, not with each other, something more mighty.
It wasn't the oceans or earthquakes, instead
Something else, which we must all fear and dread.
They told us toleration was no longer an option.
For they'd seen enough, and come to the conclusion.
We would not be allowed to continue, on this ruinous course.
They had pondered and conversed, but now with remorse.
They would end it themselves, as they decided was their right.
They would stand by, no longer, watching us fight.
Like bad little children. But they feared, an option no longer confiscation.
No sympathy at all, it would mean almost eradication!
They would spare all the children and those good of heart,
But all the others they feared must depart.
They would be taken away to a universe so far.
They would live on a planet near the Cirrus star.
With no need for weapons and no need for money.
But neither a planet full of milk and honey.
They would live out their lives with time to reflect
On how to lead a better life, fair and correct.
Depending on each other for food and for drink.
And if they couldn't? Well they would sink!
Our family turned to us now. The artists the poets
And said with a smile you are our true brothers, tho' you did not know it!
We put you on this Earth in the hopes you would flourish.
Hoping all the others you'd eventually abolish.

But sadly your task became too large to handle
And tho' we thought long and deeply, not to meddle.
We had to take action to help with your dilemma.
You are not to blame, just those with an evil agenda.
Now go forth in peace and let your talents flow.
Teach the children to care, love and respect, and above all to know.
Of this day. When their family returned to right all the wrongs,
Paint it on canvas, teach it in poetry, and write it in songs.
So that they may not forget it, so they will not stray.
For fear, once again, we will come back some day!
I woke up this morning and turned on the TV
Wars, famine, another family butchered I see.
I turn off the TV, with a long drawn out sigh.
Will we ever learn? I fear not unless we at least try!
I fear for our future it really looks sad
With our fates it seems, in the hands of the bad.
But just maybe one day our family will return, I hope and pray.
On the other hand they could already be here, amongst us, they may.
And when the day arrives when they make themselves known.
The Evil ones in the land? Well their seeds are already sown.
They will reap their crop; they will all get their dues.
A life of remorse and guilt. Perhaps death they may choose?
Until that day comes my friends, do not despair.
Don't fall into a rage, or tear at your hair.
Smile that knowing smile and just do your best
Spread the word spread your love to all of the rest

The Future?

There came a violent rapping on my door the other day,
A dark suited gentleman said “I’ve brought a guest here to stay”.
I looked in surprise, aghast and made known my distain.
He whispered, “Could we come in? I think it’s now going to rain”.
We obviously needed to talk so I bade them, “Come in please!”
The chap looked quite bedraggled and let out a sneeze.
“Pray tell what have I done to deserve this reward?”
“But I must say it’s come at the right time, I’m feeling quite bored!”
“Because your unemployed , over-qualified and over the hill”.
“It’s part of a Government initiative, two birds with one stone to kill!”
Puzzled and dumbfounded, I scratched my head and furrowed my brow.
“I don’t want to appear stupid!” I said “But I quite fail to see how!”
“It’s quite simple” he said “Your job is to show him our customs and ways”,
“Teach him basic English, the currency, make him comfortable, so he stays”
“And if I don’t care to?” I asked , fearing my friends’ sheer derisions.
“Then, I’m afraid about your benefits, we’ll be forced to make decisions!”
I knew what he meant, by the snide sneer on his face.
He’d quickly, officially but sneakily, put me firmly in my place.
“Just help him fill in these forms, being totally precise and honest”.
With that he dropped them on the table, half a Brazilian rain forest!
He snatched up his black briefcase, with an insignia upon it.
“Goodbye and good luck, just show your true British grit!”
I looked around at the poor dishevelled stranger, dumbfounded.
The pen pushing bureaucrat, had left me totally astounded.
“What is your name?” I asked, hoping he was understanding.
He just stood and stared, not a clue just listening.
It was plain to anyone that this was not underhand.
He wasn’t putting it on, truly didn’t understand.
Not a word of English could he convert or relate,

And by now I was sweating and getting in quite a state.
We turned to hand signals and long drawn out words.
I taught him about Pelican crossings, he, me, about the Kurds.
I cooked him chicken and chips, roast beef 'n' Yorkshire pud.
He tried showing me how to make Couscous, I never understood.
We had battles with the radio, our music tastes didn't match.
I wanted Classic Pop, he'd turn it to R&B, mainly 'Dolla Sign Snatch'.
I came home one day my furnishings and décor' looked strange.
Hues of wild colours, cushions on the floor, hardly 'G-Plan' range.
A month or two later his friends and relatives had moved in.
God knows where they all slept, didn't care, I was now on the Gin!
Two weeks later and rent overdue, I was told I would have to move out.
"We need more room", Knapsack on my back, I left quietly without a shout.
I'm now one of Sally's Army, 'no fixed abode', so no longer any dole.
I sit all day a tin at my feet, a sign saying "please give if you've any soul."
A man walking by, looked down with disgust at my dishevelled state.
Saying, "If he'd any pride he wouldn't be begging!" to his copycat mate.
I looked up at him, the memory came flooding back, but alas no loot.
It was my officious friend, the man in the smart expensive dark suit.

Eyes Wide Shut

Come with me truly look not a cursory glance.

Tarry a moment inhale, just take your chance.

It may be your last, you never do know,

Because what we all reap we eventually sow

Our ‘mother’ is slowly dying bit by precious bit,

If we do not take care we won’t be able to stop it.

We rape and burden her without care or thought.

Not thinking, to beyond the saturation point we’ve brought.

It’s nearly too late, can you not hear the piteous screams?

We all carry on heads down ears and eyes closed, it seems!

Look around at your world a wonderful miraculous place.

Why do you choose to ignore it, not to look in its face?

Its beauty fading fast, as tiredness now takes over.

Ignored and well worn like a rejected lover.

But love her again we must for the time to turn may be lost,

We have all harvested the benefits, now we must pay the cost.

Put aside the greed, carelessness and wanton destruction.

Time to use our reasoning and powers of deduction.

Cut down on the terrible waste, the over farming and fishing,

The wasteful burning and spillage of fuels, the wars and the hurt.

We must begin to speak our minds, say no, and learn to be curt.

If we do not and continue to walk about with eyes wide shut.

We will be no more, there will not be an if, and, or but!

The Fear of It

Getting my 'five a day' seems quite a big ask.

It's turned into a chore, it's setting me a task.

But at least I'm getting my much needed vitamin C,

How I managed before, I just cannot see.

But now because of all that extra acid.

With the care of my teeth I cannot be placid.

I must now brush them after every meal.

If I don't, I fear their fate I will seal.

They, while I'm talking, will drop out to the floor.

Roll along the carpet and out of the door.

If my shirt gets splashed with soup, maybe Chowder?

I can't just wash it with my usual powder.

To use a biological genius would be the best.

Costs a little more, but no stains left on your vest.

And when I'm chucking-out the everyday rubbish bag

I must section it all, and sort it, not let my feet drag.

A place for paper and cardboard, separate for plastic and tin.

If I don't I'll incur a fine, and a refusal to take my contaminated bin.

Next a letter from the bank, telling me to mind my P's and Q's.

Don't dare overdraw, if it's **their** bank you want to use.

But if you do because it's just something you can't surmount.

They will be forced to charge you some ridiculously vast amount.

The news on the telly tells of another MP taking some flack,

Don't worry though we'll soon forget because of a terrorist attack.

Watch what you eat, because it may have a genetic modification,

You wouldn't want to become two headed, a ridiculous situation.

Hiding away from the world to your bedroom you'd scurry.

And what's worse than that? Now twice as much worry!

All this care we must take, does not well for our future bode.

But panic not for any day now, I've heard the planet will explode!

The Star

Jim sat
The ground giving
No favour to his old brittle bones
The coloured lights shone brightly all around
Sweet smells, Cinnamon floating on air. Bells ringing, a wondrous sound
Children giggling, arguing, shouting out loud
Parents smiling, but worrying, presents to be found, kids lost in the crowd.
Jim sits on his throne, shivering, but smiling and patiently rattling his tin,"Spare a
penny Guv?"
Man too busy turns a deaf ear, looks away without love
Jim just smiles, knowing, not wanting the fuss, doesn't hate, doesn't judge, just
hopes.
Children laughing, throwing snow balls, building snowmen, trying out sledges on
slippery slopes.
Santa Ho! Ho! Ho!..ing, Mulled wine in the stores for the people buying.
Smiling assistants, dressed in seasonal garb, red furry caps trimmed with white fur
Loud noises from the fountain of chocolate, drunken Jesters acting foolish, causing
quite a stir.
Jim looks on smiling, memories flooding back, pulls his rags tightly round.
Snow starts to fall people cheer with delight
"Come on kids, let's get home, guess who's coming tonight
A can rattles meekly "Spare a penny guv?"
"No change!" were replies
"Merry Christmas Guv!"

A toothless smile on his wind battered face.
“His fault! He shouldn’t have fallen from grace!”
He looked at the faces all scurrying and hurrying by
All in a hurry, invisible to them! He didn’t need to try.
Warmth left his body swiftly, through his tattered rags,
A hand touched, as he rose up slowly gathering his bags
“Ready Jim? Did you think we’d forsake you on this holy night?”
Jim stepped into his carriage, full of sounds, happiness and glee
And there on the dash board stood, lit with a tiny star, a small Christmas tree
With a verse just below it, in letters bright red. ‘Merry Christmas and good health to
you one and all’.
For let us remember, Christmas is not just for us, but also for people, who
unfortunately hit the wall!
Merry Xmas

Four Square Metre World

Lace, billowing gossamer against my four square metre world.

A time machine, as I watch the world sweep by, lost in fear.

Hurrying here and hurrying there, heads held down against the clock.

Worrying about the payments overdue, the politician's grimy smile.

Had I not the old father upon my back, I would wipe off that grin.

Could I but stir these weary work worn, once strong pillars.

I would stride up to the hilltops and shout enough! Release them!

They would fear my wrath and I would build an army of like souls.

We would defeat them at every advance and push out into the blue.

Taking back our rights and freedom of soul, cowering no more.

But standing straight, erect looking each other in the eye knowing.

All anxious thoughts dissolved running away through time.

We would all become warriors of peace, become one, unafraid at last.

Lace, billowing gossamer against my four square metre world.

Memories Residing

Oh to lay me down in fields of golden wheat prostrate,
Watching cotton clouds cross azure blue skies and abate.
Helios gazing down, warming me with tender, gentle care.
Hawk on high, stalling and climbing, but ever watchful stare.
Stone like decent, silent and deadly end to tiny mouse or shrew.
To see old man beetle, dashing by, rushing where, if only he knew.
Sitting upon rocks, as squabbling water tumbles by, o'er pebble gems.
Flowing forth, with excitement and glee, down hills and glens.
Clean and crisp babbling stream, proffering cheek, for icy kiss.
Pure, newborn anew, promise of life, giving succour and earth bliss.
Seeing a miracle, a birth, a lamb, a completion of cyclic life,
Gambolling gangly fools, celebrating, no fear of the butcher's knife.
Walking velvet, newly mown meadow, ambrosia rivalled by few.
Carpets of purple-blue velvet and gold, labouring with dew.
Aromas flooding senses, as blooms and herbs compete to win favours.
Insects, called, obey, enraptured by delicious, scented flavours.
The earthy odours of fresh turned soil, gently stinging nostrils wide.
Chastising Seagulls, flocking to the plough and forgetting the tide.
Bushes of Blackbirds warbling chorus, sharp, true and bright.
The Judas Cuckoo, trying to compete, as the Skylark takes flight,
High aloft to heaven she climbs, all but out of sight, a fluttering speck.
To out-fox the Fox, the Weasel and Stoat, her clutch unguarded upon the deck.
She sings her song of deft deceit, completing distraction, a clever tool.
Then danger past, she floats down, several yards adrift, again to fool.

She zig-zags, towards the nest, where waits her mate, the last defence.
The fox trots by, the ruse worked, he'd seen the bird, knew not whence.
Dusk veiled hedgerows, silhouettes of black against a Shepherd's sky, render.
Orange grove clouds, tear the even skies asunder, with resultant vista splendour.
Gnats dance like fools, with gay abandon, swirling around a wafted hand.
Grasshoppers, rubbing legs on wings, Nightjars join chorus, for the evening's band.
I lay my head on downy pillow, watching through open window now,
Awaiting Morpheus, drinking in the night, and all that the day did bestow.

www.ingramcontent.com/pod-product-compliance
Ingram Content Group UK Ltd.
Pitfield, Milton Keynes, MK11 3LW, UK
UKHW020233250726
13967UKWH00001B/339